GW00746394

Analogue Guide

Berlin

Contents

Berlin

—Welcome to Analogue Berlin

Berlin is probably the most happening city in Europe today and certainly the most fascinating of the continent's major capitals. Its cityscape is punctured by reminders of its location at the fault line of Europe's Atlanticist West and what Russia has deemed its backyard. Over the past hundred years alone, Berlin has played the role of capital of an audacious monarchy, a progressive democracy, a world-domination-seeking dictatorship, a socialist model state, and seat of a modern Germany that sees itself irrefutably linked to its European neighbours.

Today the physical scars of the city's partition have been paved over and are barely noticeable. The German government has reclaimed its seat around the Reichstag, and newcomer West Germans attest that vandalism and other big city evils are largely in check. Berlin is once more at the centre of Germany's cultural and creative scenes, and its cheap rents have turned it into a magnet for young artistic types from across the globe. In fact, there is talk that Berlin may have become so successful at being "poor but sexy" that it is about to be taken over by the bourgeoisie.

Undoubtedly a more mainstream city than it was two decades ago, Berlin's unique history has left it with a diverse set of neighbourhoods, architecture and people. In the former East, Mitte has dramatically shifted from socialist decay to the embodiment of contemporary Berlin, boasting innovative retail and a vibrant art and café scene. In the West, Charlottenburg and Schöneberg exude the air of prosperous 20th century West Germany.

We've set out to chart the best of what this unparalleled city has to offer, with photography and maps throughout. Enjoy!

Neighbourhoods

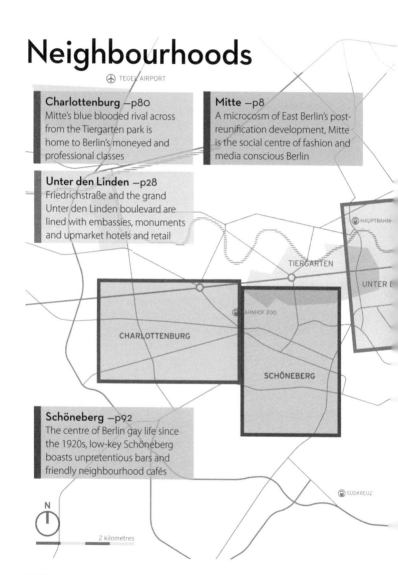

TEGEL AIRPORT

Charlottenburg —p80
Mitte's blue blooded rival across from the Tiergarten park is home to Berlin's moneyed and professional classes

Mitte —p8
A microcosm of East Berlin's post-reunification development, Mitte is the social centre of fashion and media conscious Berlin

Unter den Linden —p28
Friedrichstraße and the grand Unter den Linden boulevard are lined with embassies, monuments and upmarket hotels and retail

HAUPTBAHN

TIERGARTEN

UNTER D

BAHNHOF ZOO

CHARLOTTENBURG

SCHÖNEBERG

Schöneberg —p92
The centre of Berlin gay life since the 1920s, low-key Schöneberg boasts unpretentious bars and friendly neighbourhood cafés

SÜDKREUZ

N

2 kilometres

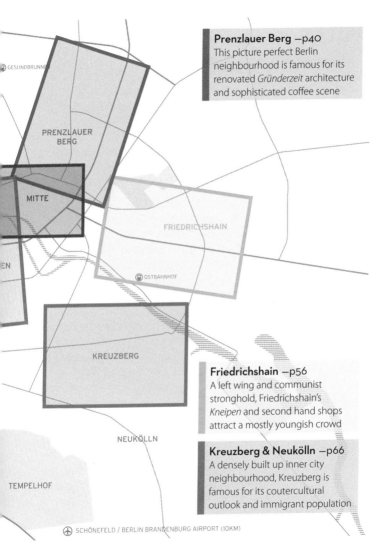

Prenzlauer Berg —p40
This picture perfect Berlin neighbourhood is famous for its renovated *Gründerzeit* architecture and sophisticated coffee scene

GESUNDBRUNNEN

PRENZLAUER BERG

MITTE

EN

FRIEDRICHSHAIN

OSTBAHNHOF

KREUZBERG

Friedrichshain —p56
A left wing and communist stronghold, Friedrichshain's *Kneipen* and second hand shops attract a mostly youngish crowd

NEUKÖLLN

Kreuzberg & Neukölln —p66
A densely built up inner city neighbourhood, Kreuzberg is famous for its coutercultural outlook and immigrant population

TEMPELHOF

SCHÖNEFELD / BERLIN BRANDENBURG AIRPORT (10KM)

Mitte

—New Centre of Urban Life

Despite accounting for a mere fraction of Berlin's historical centre, the former Spandauer Vorstadt is what is commonly referred to as "Mitte" today. As the largest contiguous part of Mitte to have survived both WWII air raids and subsequent socialist town planning, the neighbourhood is a microcosm of East Berlin's post-reunification development from communist bleakness to fashion and media conscious metropolis.

The Spandauer Vorstadt, the suburb north of Berlin's former city walls, dates back to the 17th century, when barns were relocated here from Berlin proper for fire safety reasons. The blocks east of Rosenthaler Straße are still known as Scheunenviertel, or "Barn District". In the 18th century, the suburb became the centre of Berlin's Jewish cultural and commercial life. Despite its location at the heart of socialist East Germany, the neglected area remained unaffected by efforts to restyle nearby Alexanderplatz as a socialist city centre. After Berlin's reunification, "Mitte" became the first part of former East Berlin to be discovered by investors and dropouts alike. Today the Hackeschen Höfe, a stunning art nouveau courtyard complex dense with retail, and the Tacheles, an art collective in the ruins of a former department store, are busy tourist attractions.

Mitte, particularly along its calmer fringes, continues to be the site of numerous art galleries and independent shops, and is increasingly upmarket. The area's southern half meanwhile has evolved into a fairly mainstream retail destination with flagship stores of international brands and white-collar offices. More avant-garde culinary and retail offerings can be found beyond Torstraße and along up-and-coming Chausseestraße and Brunnenstraße.

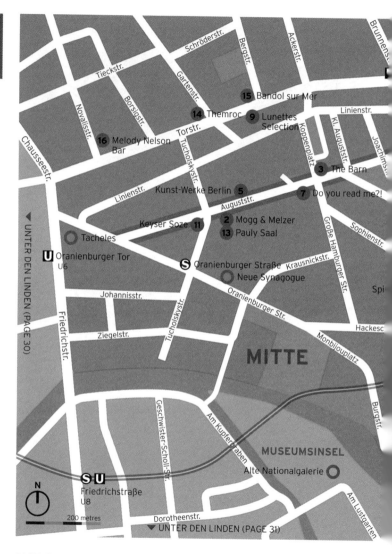

15 Bandol sur Mer

14 Themroc 9 Lunettes Selection

16 Melody Nelson Bar

3 The Barn

Kunst-Werke Berlin 5

7 Do you read me?!

Keyser Soze 11 2 Mogg & Melzer
13 Pauly Saal

Tacheles

U Oranienburger Tor
U6

S Oranienburger Straße

Neue Synagoge

Johannisstr.

Ziegelstr.

MITTE

MUSEUMSINSEL

Alte Nationalgalerie

S U Friedrichstraße
U8

200 metres

▲ UNTER DEN LINDEN (PAGE 30)

▼ UNTER DEN LINDEN (PAGE 31)

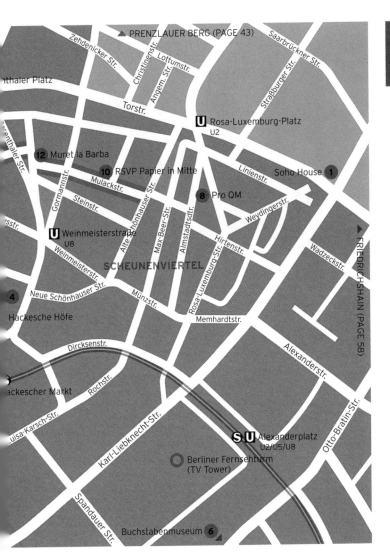

PRENZLAUER BERG (PAGE 43)

Zehdenicker Str.

Christinenstr.

Lottumstr.

Angem. Str.

Saarbrücker Str.

Straßburger Str.

...thaler Platz

Torstr.

U Rosa-Luxemburg-Platz
U2

...enthaler Str.

12 Muret la Barba

10 RSVP Papier in Mitte

Linienstr.

Soho House **1**

Gormannstr.

Mulackstr.

Steinstr.

Alte Schönhauser Str.

Max-Beer-Str.

Almstadtstr.

8 Pro QM

Weydingerstr.

...sstr.

U Weinmeisterstraße
U8

Weinmeisterstr.

SCHEUNENVIERTEL

Hirtenstr.

Rosa-Luxemburg-Str.

Wadzeckstr.

FRIEDRICHSHAIN (PAGE 58)

4

Neue Schönhauser Str.

Münzstr.

Hackesche Höfe

Memhardtstr.

Alexanderstr.

Dircksenstr.

Rochstr.

...ackescher Markt

...uisa-Karsch-Str.

Karl-Liebknecht-Str.

Otto-Bratin-Str.

S U Alexanderplatz
U2/U5/U8

Berliner Fernsehturm
(TV Tower)

Spandauer Str.

Buchstabenmuseum **6**

Members' Club and Hotel

Soho House

Torstraße 1
+49 30 4050440
sohohouseberlin.de
Rosa-Luxemburg-Platz **U2**,
Alexanderplatz **S** **U2** **U5** **U8**
Doubles from €150/night incl. tax

Occupying a majestic 1928 Bauhaus structure, the Berlin branch of UK-based members' club Soho House offers plush lodgings half way between Mitte and Prenzlauer Berg. The building's multiple historical functions mirror recent Berlin history. Over the past ninety odd years it has morphed from upscale Jewish-owned department store to Hitler Youth HQ to Communist Party archive to the cosmopolitan club and hotel that it is today. The hotel's rooftop pool and restaurant, Cookhouse, offer stunning views of the city.

Stylish Deli

Mogg & Melzer

 Auguststraße 11-13
+49 30 33006070
maedchenschule.org
Oranienburger Straße $\bigcirc$,
Oranienburger Tor **U6**, Rosenthaler
Platz **U8**
Open daily. Mon-Fri 8am-10pm; Sat/
Sun 10am-10pm.

Housed in the same *Jüdische Mädschenschule* (Jewish Girl's School) as restaurant Pauly Saal (p24), Oskar Melzer and Paul Mogg's refined delicatessen merges European design classics with inspiration from 1930s New York. With views of Mitte's picturesque Auguststraße outside its generous windows, the deli is an excellent spot to grab breakfast, lunch or *Kaffee und Kuchen* before hitting Mitte's countless shops and galleries.

Beans with a Provenance

The Barn

3 Auguststraße 58
+49 151 24105136
thebarn.de
Rosenthaler Platz **U8**,
Oranienburger Straße **S**
Closed Mon. Open Tue-Fri 8:30am-6pm; Sat/Sun 10am-6pm.

The Barn is a quality driven café and roaster in the thick of Mitte's independent boutiques and galleries. Espousing a coffee philosophy based on the importance of the link between micro-farmer, specialty roaster and individual coffee shop, The Barn delves deep into the origins of its sumptuous beans. The café's décor is chic-barn-minimalist and floor to ceiling windows allow for ample street watching while you imbibe.

Asanas Overlooking the Alex

Spirit Yoga

 Rosenthaler Straße 36
+49 30 27908503

spirityoga.de

Weinmeisterstraße **U8**, Hackescher Markt **S**

Classes daily. Classes from €13; showers on premises.

A sun-drenched *vinyasa*-style yoga studio, Spirit Yoga boasts ample studio space and stunning views of the emblematic Alex TV tower reigning over Mitte. The studio's extensive schedule includes classes ranging from pre-natal to power lunch yoga and pilates. Classes in English are offered a few times a week. Spirit Yoga has a second location in Charlotteburg (see map p83).

Artistic Vanguard

Kunst-Werke Berlin

 Auguststraße 69
+49 30 243459
kw-berlin.de
Oranienburger Straße Ⓢ,
Rosenthaler Platz U8
Closed Tue. Open Wed-Mon noon-
7pm; Thu noon-9pm. Admission €6

An independent cultural entity, KW Centre for Contemporary Art exhibits, commissions, and produces contemporary art that explores issues relevant to today's international society. Established in the 1990s by Klaus Biesenbach in a derelict margarine factory, KW has been at the vanguard of Berlin's art scene since the fall of the Berlin Wall. In addition to exhibitions, performances and talks, the gallery boasts courtyard Café Bravo, a convivial spot to sip on an *Apfelschorle* while enjoying the Mitte vibe.

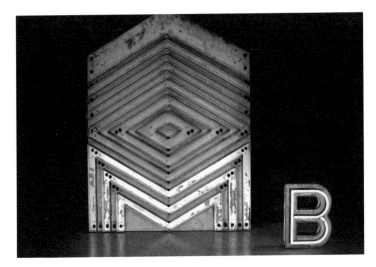

Gutenberg's Legacy

Buchstabenmuseum

⑥ Holzmarktstraße 66
+49 177 4201587
buchstabenmuseum.de
Jannowitzbrücke Ⓢ U8,
Klosterstraße U2
Closed Mon-Wed. Open Thu-Sun
1pm-5pm. Admission €6.50

Germany is home to print, from Gutenberg to modern typeface luminaries. For the lover of typography, the "Letter Museum" assembles stellar letterforms and typographic objects in its highly original collection. From an outstanding rendition of the "U" from the U-Bahn to an "M" from the Markthalle with a distinct patina, the letters are taken out of context, allowing them to appropriate new meanings and to be admired in their uncorrupted state.

Avant-garde Press

Do you read me?!

 Auguststraße 28
+49 30 69549695
doyoureadme.de
Rosenthaler Platz **U8**,
Oranienburger Straße **S**
Closed Sun. Open Mon-Sat 10am-7.30pm.

Located in a well-appointed space in one of Mitte's most intriguing retail pockets, Do you read me?! provides a floor-to-ceiling range of cutting edge international press and avant-garde and niche print. Delve into an expansive selection of titles spanning but not limited to art, culture, architecture, design and society. Once you've stocked up on printed matter, why not head over to The Barn (p14) to fire up your intellect with an espresso.

The Intellectual City

Pro QM

8 Almstadtstraße 48-50
+49 30 24728520
pro-qm.de
Rosa-Luxemburg-Platz **U2**,
Weinmeisterstraße **U8**
Closed Sun. Open Mon-Sat 11am-8pm.

An enthralling thematic bookshop founded by a trio of artist/architect/art-theorists, Pro QM focuses on the city and its relation to politics, pop culture, economic critique, architecture, design and art. Mountains of colourful publications elegantly cascade down the shop's walls and iron staircase. The lofty space was designed in the 1920s by the office of Modernist architect Hans Poelzigin and maintains a breezy feel highly conducive to browsing. Honing in on Pro QM's interdisciplinary design focus, intellectually charged talks and events are regularly held.

Mint Vintage Specs

Lunettes Selection

 Torstraße 172
+49 30 20215216
lunettes-selection.de
Rosenthaler Platz **U8**,
Oranienburger Straße **S**
Closed Sun. Open Mon/Tue/Th/
Fri noon-8pm; Wed 10am-8pm; Sat
noon-6pm.

Sumptuous vintage eyewear
shop Lunettes Selection stocks an
expertly curated range of refined
specs and shades refurbished to
mint condition. A visit to the shop
goes beyond the merely chic by
offering the patron a unique walk
through optical history. Styles
run the gamut from *belle époque*
classics to mid-century cool and
1980s aviator. Show off your new
acquisition pavement-side at Keyser
Soze (p22) while quaffing a glass of
Riesling.

Stationary from across the Globe

RSVP Papier in Mitte

10 Mulackstraße 14
+49 30 28094644
rsvp-berlin.de
Weinmeisterstraße **U8**, Rosa-
Luxemburg-Platz **U2**
Closed Sun. Open Mon-Thu noon-
7pm; Fri/Sat noon-8pm.

An elegant modern *papiterie* in a
cosy pocket of Mitte, RSVP Papier
stocks a well curated selection of
writing paraphernalia, including
a comprehensive range of
home-grown luxurious writing
instruments from Usus Berlin and
Kaweco. The shop's offerings extend
further afield to incorporate diaries
from Korea, notebooks from Japan
and papers from Portugal, to name
but a few.

When in Mitte...

Keyser Soze

 Tucholskystr. 33
+49 30 28599489

keyser-soze.de

Oranienburger Straße **S**,
Oranienburger Tor **U6**,Rosenthaler
Platz **U8**

Open daily 7.30am-3am.

A quirky Mitte institution, Keyser Soze's pavement-side banquettes famously spill over into the neighbourhood streetscape. Home cooking is on offer throughout the day, as are coffee, cake and a range of drinks. Kick back with a refreshing *Berliner Pilsener* and instantly become part of the Mitte scene.

Vini e Capuccini

Muret la Barba

 Rosenthaler Straße 61
+49 30 28097212
muretlabarba.de
Rosenthaler Platz **U8**, Rosa-
Luxemburg-Platz **U2**
Open daily. Mon-Fri 10am-midnight;
Sat/Sun noon-midnight.

Wedged on one of Mitte's most charming corners, Muret la Barba introduced Berlin to the innovative concept of in-house wine retailer within a fabulous wine bar and restaurant. Take your bottle home at retail price or pay a modest corkage fee to imbibe in-house, with or without Muret's fresh Italian fare. The restaurant's bubbly, urbane ambiance and eclectic crowd make it a great spot for a casual meal.

Elegant Cafeteria

Pauly Saal

 Auguststraße 11
+49 30 33006070
paulysaal.com
Oranienburger Straße **S**,
Rosenthaler Platz **U8**
Closed Sun. Open Mon-Sat noon-3pm, 8pm-3am.

A cavernous and meticulously appointed gem of a restaurant, Pauly Saal is located in what was originally the *Jüdische Mädschenschule*'s (Jewish Girls School) cafeteria. Inventive spins on local and regional classics such as smoked eel with caviar and Pomeranian ox entrecote are executed with panache. A meaty affair through and through, an elegantly stuffed fox watches over diners from its perch, while a discharged rocket ship sits squarely above the kitchen.

Jewel on the Torstraße

Themroc

14 Torstraße 183
+49 30 2824474
themroc-berlin.de
Oranienburger Straße Ⓢ,
Rosenthaler Platz U8
Open daily 7pm-2am.

A bijou culinary gem on Torstraße, the bustling divider between Mitte and Prenzlauer Berg, Themroc's daily French-inspired menu is as inventive (and concise) as it is delicious. Inside, the unassuming space is appointed with a cosy wood-and-marble bar, high ceilings and fresh cut flowers. During the summer months, tables spill out onto the street making for convivial *al fresco* dining.

Quircky Gastronomy

Bandol sur Mer

15 Torstraße 167
+49 30 76302052
bandolsurmer.de
Rosenthaler Platz **U8**,
Oranienburger Straße **S**
Open daily 6pm-11pm.

Bandol offers *prix-fixe* menus comprising several courses of refined and stylised French-inspired cuisine in a playful setting. Popular with members of the creative industries and foodies seeking a laid back approach to high calibre gastronomy, Bandol pulls off cuisine with quirky aplomb. A few outdoor tables are laid out over the warmer months, adding to the *plaisir* of it all.

Cocktail Bar

Melody Nelson Bar

 Oranienburger Straße 54
+49 30 2826185
Oranienburger Tor **U6**,
Oranienburger Straße **S**
Open daily. Sun-Thu 8pm-2am; Fri/
Sat 8am-4am.

For an evening of cocktails, smokes
and lugubrious conversation in a
former Stasi hangout, head to the
dark and attractive Franco-German
co-production Melody Nelson Bar.
Order your dry martini and snuggle
into a comfy sofa while basking
in the limelight of an overblown
portrait of Jane Birkin, the voice
behind Serge Gainsbourg's 1971
cult album, *Histoire de Melody
Nelson*.

Unter den Linden

—Grand Historical City Centre

The grand Unter den Linden boulevard connects Berlin's former Old Town with the Brandenburg Gate in the West. The area around it is the site of government buildings, embassies, department stores, operas—Berlin has three—and bold monuments to the those who have governed Germany from here.

Berlin dates back to 1237, the earliest mention of a fishing village named Cölln on the site of today's Museum Island. In the 17th century, Prussia's Hohenzollern rulers transformed the bridle path connecting the city with the Tiergarten hunting grounds into the glamorous Unter den Linden boulevard and developed the suburb of Friedrichstadt on the adjacent lands. Meticulous planning and royal stewardship provided grand public buildings and ensured wealthy residents. Merged into Berlin, the 19th century Friedrichstadt became Germany's financial centre and the city's business and entertainment district. During the Cold War, heavily damaged Mitte was the centre of East Berlin. Beyond repair, Berlin's medieval old town was replaced with a modern socialist city centre around wind-swept Alexanderplatz and its famous "Alex" TV tower. The Stadtschloss, the former royal residence, made way for the now dismantled Palace of the Republic, which, aside from its rubber-stamp parliament, also boasted a bowling alley and a discotheque.

After Berlin's reunification, Mitte quickly reclaimed its role as the political and cultural centre of the country. The area around Friedrichstraße and elegant Gendarmenmarkt boasts upmarket shops and luxurious hotels. Potsdamer Platz was redeveloped from a no man's land to today's popular, though bland, commercial district. Further east, socialist Alexanderplatz (map p11) has been taken over by national retail brands.

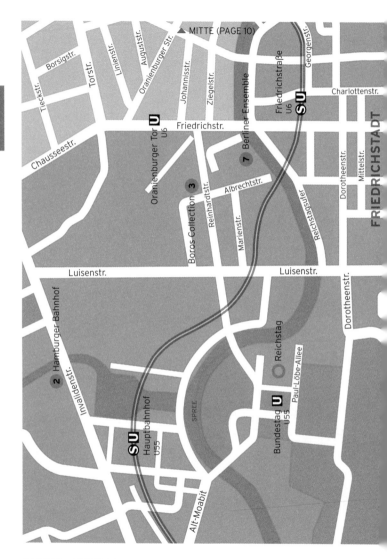

FRIEDRICHSTADT

Borsigstr.

Tieckstr.

Torstr.

Linienstr.

Oranienburger Str.

Auguststr.

Johannisstr.

Ziegelstr.

Friedrichstraße
U6

Georgenstr.

Charlottenstr.

Chausseestr.

U Friedrichstr.

Oranienburger Tor
U6

S U

3 Boros Collection

Reinhardtstr.

Albrechtstr.

7 Berliner Ensemble

Dorotheenstr.

Mittelstr.

Marienstr.

Reichstagsufer

Luisenstr.

Luisenstr.

Dorotheenstr.

2 Hamburger Bahnhof

Invalidenstr.

Reichstag

S U Hauptbahnhof
U55

SPREE

U Bundestag
U55

Paul-Löbe-Allee

Alt-Moabit

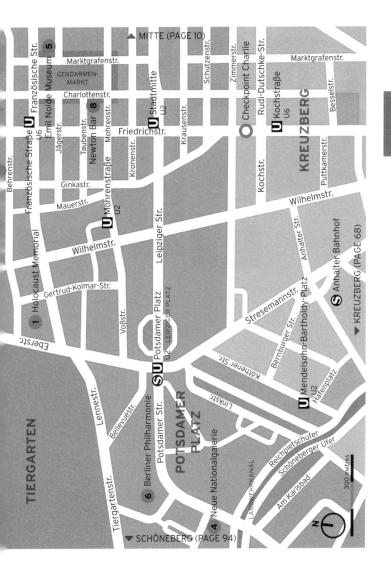

Commemorative Structure

Holocaust Memorial

1 Cora-Berliner-Straße
+49 30 26394336
stiftung-denkmal.de
Brandenburger Tor ⑤ U55
Public access. Place of Information:
Closed Mon. Open Tue-Sun 10am-
8pm (winter 10am-7pm).
Free admission.

Located one block south of Brandenburg Gate, the Peter Eisenman designed memorial to the Jewish victims of the Holocaust is made of 2,711 concrete slabs, or stelae, arranged in a grid pattern on a sloping field. The site's fringes are open to the surrounding streets, yet upon entering the structure engulfs its visitors, creating an uneasily quiet atmosphere. An underground "Place of Information" serves as a museum and holds the names of all known Jewish Holocaust victims.

Art Station

Hamburger Bahnhof

 Invalidenstraße 50
+49 30 39783411
hamburgerbahnhof.de
Hauptbahnhof ⓈⓊ55
Closed Mon. Open Tue/Wed/Fri-Sun
10am-6pm; Thu 10am-8pm.
Admission €10

The third, contemporary, component of Berlin's Nationalgalerie (see also p35), Hamburger Bahnhof is located in a mid-19th century Neoclassical former train station. Its stately façade and cavernous installations make for a dramatic backdrop for work at the vanguard of interdisciplinary contemporary art from the 1960s to the present. The museum's Marx collection includes Andy Warhol's oversized portrait of Mao while Giacometti's sculptures are on display as part of the Friedrich Christian Flick collection.

Art Collection in a Bunker

Boros Collection

 Reinhardtstraße 20
+49 30 27594065
boros.de
Oranienburger Tor **U6**,
Friedrichstraße **S** **U6**
Closed Mon-Wed. Open Thu-Sun
10am-6pm. Prebooked tours only.
Admission €12

Located in a dramatic converted WWII bunker that once served as a textile factory, the Boros Collection is a gargantuan private assemblage of international contemporary art, spread over eighty exhibition rooms. Given its epic proportions, the collection is shown in phases, with work across media from the early 90s and recent acquisitions currently on display. The artists install their work and several installations incorporate sound, making for a multisensory experience.

Kandinsky and Mies

Neue Nationalgalerie

4 Herbert-von-Karajan-Straße 1
+49 30 254880
berliner-philharmoniker.de
Potsdamer Platz **S U2**
Closed Mon. Open Tue/Wed/Fri
10am-6pm; Thu 10am-8pm; Sat/Sun
11am-6pm. Admission €10

Mies van der Rohe's bold steel and glass clear-span structure provides stunning backdrop to Berlin's most comprehensive collection of early 20th century Modern art. While the museum's collection of Picassos and Kandiskys certainly warrant a visit in of themselves, Mies' building and sculpture garden are at least as intriguing.

Nolde's Urban Experience

Emil Nolde Museum

 Jägerstraße 55
+49 30 40 00 46 90
nolde-stiftung.de
Hausvogteiplatz **U2**, Französische
Straße **U6**
Open daily 10am-7pm. Admission €8

Emil Nolde's highly expressive oil and watercolour paintings capture the essence of both his native windswept Schleswig, on the German-Danish border, and of the Berlin of cabarets and masked balls that he and his wife Ada called home every winter from 1905 onwards. An extension of the Emil Nolde Foundation in Seebüll, the Berlin museum offers insight into the artist's less frequently explored urban experience.

Premier Concert Venue

Berliner Philharmonie

6 Herbert-von-Karajan-Straße 1
+49 30 254880
berliner-philharmoniker.de
Potsdamer Platz **S** **U2**
Regular performances. Refer to
website for programme.

The Berlin Philharmonic Orchestra's home base is an early 1960s hall designed by Hans Scharoun. The structure is acclaimed for its pioneering architecture and acoustics, and was the first concert hall to incorporate vineyard-style seating, with terraces rising on all sides from a central stage—a prime vantage point from which to view and hear one of Europe's premier classical orchestras.

Brecht's Theatre

Berliner Ensemble

 Bertolt-Brecht-Platz 1
+49 30 28408
berliner-ensemble.de
Friedrichstraße S U6
Regular performances. Refer to
website for programme.

Home to Bertolt Brecht's Berliner Ensemble since 1954, the Theater am Schiffbauerdamm was also the site of the original 1928 staging of the playwright's Three Penny Opera. The theatre's plush Neo-baroque interior and Spree-side location off Friedrichstrasse heighten the magic of the repertoire on offer, which, in addition to Brecht's work, includes plays by Thomas Bernhard, Max Frisch and Samuel Beckett.

Nude on the Rocks

Newton Bar

 Charlottenstraße 57
+49 30 20295421

newton-bar.de

Französische Straße **U6**,
Stadtmitte **U2** **U6**

Open daily. Thu-Sat 10am-4am; Sun-
Wed 10am-3am.

Decked out in red leather, marble and, of course, original Helmut Newton black-and-white nudes, this plush and sexy 1960s-glam bar lives up to its namesake's reputation. Swing by for a stiff drink and some conversation while admiring the eclectic mix of patrons with a twinkle of the eye.

Prenzlauer Berg
—Perfect Neighbourhood

Prenzlauer Berg is widely regarded as the perfect Berlin neighbourhood: swathes of renovated *Gründerzeit* apartment buildings sit atop a vibrant street life and sophisticated coffee scene. Formerly East Germany's intellectual hub, and bohemian well into the 1990s, the area's popularity now extends to media executives and professionals.

Prenzlauer Berg is named after the hill on the road north from Berlin to Prenzlau. Rural until the 19th century, its farmers diversified into brewing, of which the expansive *Kulturbrauerei* cultural centre and Prater beer garden on Kastanienallee are vivid reminders. Envisioned as a working class district, Prenzlauer Berg soon developed a distinct intellectual bent; Gustav Langenscheidt founded his dictionary publishing company here. The area also had a large Jewish population who moved here from the nearby Scheunenviertel (see p8). The synagogue on Rykestraße is Germany's largest today. Left intact by World War II, but neglected by East Germany's communist government, Prenzlauer Berg fell into the hands of artists and students, primarily those opposed to the regime.

The neighbourhood's busy core is the junction at Eberswalder Straße U-Bahn, known as "Ecke Schönhauser" (corner of Schönhauser Allee). This is where bustling Kastanienallee, a popular tourist haunt, crosses the thoroughfare of Schönhauser Allee. Most of Prenzlauer Berg's culinary attractions can be found south of here and towards Mitte. The pretty residential streets to the east of Schönhauser Allee have gained a reputation for their "Swabian" (read West German), pram-pushing upmarket newcomers. Here, urban village life revolves around the outdoor cafés and weekly markets of picturesque Kollwitzplatz and Helmholtzplatz.

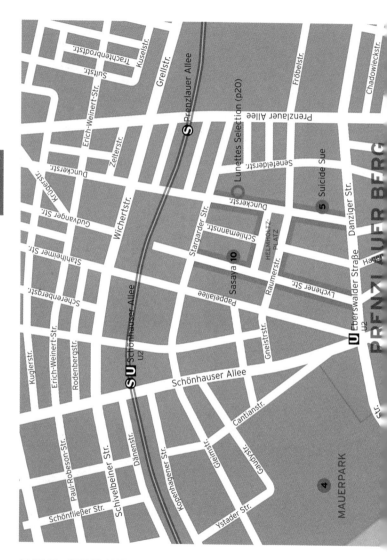

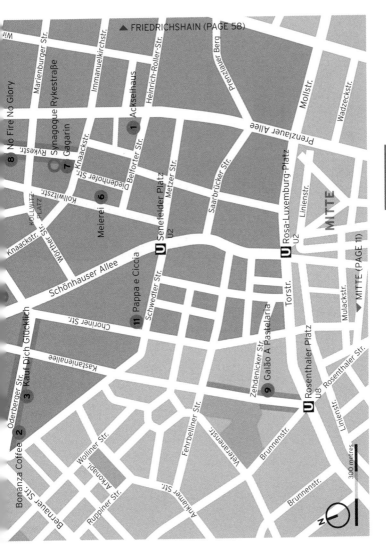

▲ FRIEDRICHSHAIN (PAGE 58)

1 Acksehaus

8 No Fire No Glory

7 Gagarin

Synagogue Rykestraße

6 Meierei

2 Bonanza Coffee

3 Kauf Dich Glücklich

11 Pappa e Ciccia

9 Galão A Pastelaria

Senefelder Platz

Rosa-Luxemburg-Platz

Rosenthaler Platz

MITTE

▶ MITTE (PAGE 11)

300 metres

A Home in Prenzlauer Berg

Acselhaus

 Belforter Straße 21
+49 30 44337633
acselhaus.de
Senefelderplatz **U2**
Doubles from €120/night incl. tax

Acselhaus is a boutique hotel in a charming pocket of Prenzlauer Berg. Housed in a restored *Gründerzeit* building surrounding a paradisiacal courtyard, each room has a distinct character. The Maritime rooms are tastefully decked out in shades of azure with luxury touches, such as comfy bathtubs and chandeliers, while the Afrika lodgings incorporate warm caramel tones and depictions of big game. Take your pick, and don't miss the excellent breakfast buffet served at the neighbouring shell-stuccoed Club del Mar.

Coffee by the Wall

Bonanza Coffee

 Oderberger Straße 35
+49 171 5630795

bonanzacoffee.de

Eberswalder Straße **U2**, Bernauer
Straße **U8**

Open daily. Mon-Fri 8.30am-7pm;
Sat/Sun 10am-7pm.

Bonanza is surely the best place to get your coffee kick on charming Oderberger Straße. With an in-house roaster and expertly trained baristas, it's no surprise that the coffee is first rate. Sit at the street-facing bar on cooler days or outside on the banquettes during warmer months. Taking your "coffee to go" to neighbouring Mauerpark (p47) isn't a bad option either.

Vintage Tea Party

Kauf Dich Glücklich

 Oderberger Straße 44
+49 30 48623292
kaufdichgluecklich.de
Eberswalder Straße **U2**, Bernauer Straße **U8**
Open daily 11am-1am.

Kauf Dich Glücklich ("Buy Yourself Happy") merges vintage bric-a-brac with an ice cream parlour-chic aesthetic. Furniture, toys and miscellaneous *objets rares* from the 1950s-70s congregate in seamlessly orchestrated serendipity around the café/shop's glam crowd of latte macchiato sipping locals. Sit at one of the colourful outdoor benches and settle in for the afternoon with a waffle and a pot of tea.

Berlin Wall Park

Mauerpark

4 between Bernauer Str and Gleimstraße

+49 30 250025

Eberswalder Straße **U2**, Bernauer Straße **U8**

Public access.

The Mauerpark, literally "Wall Park", is a vast, refreshingly vacant, expanse on the edge of Prenzlauer Berg. Formerly a rail freight yard, the site was vacated for the Berlin Wall and its broad "death strip". Preserved from encroaching development by local residents, the park has become a colourful medley of Berlin life, including joggers and jugglers, and the famous Sunday afternoon "Bearpit" karaoke show. Further west along Bernauer Straße stands the Berlin Wall Documentation Centre, which includes a 60-metre section of the former border.

Brunch to Die for

Suicide Sue

 Dunckerstraße 2
+49 30 64834745

suicidesue.com

Eberswalder Straße **U2**, Prenzlauer Allee **S**

Open daily. Mon-Fri 8am-7pm; Sat 9am-6pm; Sun 10am-7pm.

This electrically charged daily-brunch standby whips up the tender *Rührei* (scrambled eggs), fresh fruit salad atop fluffy pancakes and delectable *caffè latte* its eclectic local clientele demands. Perennially popular at the weekend, Suicide Sue's outdoor lounge-style seating fills with throngs of die-hard devotees during peak brunch hours.

Knödel and Kuchen

Meierei

 Kollwitzstraße 42
+49 30 92129573
meierei.net
Senefelderplatz **U2**
Open daily. Mon-Fri 8am-7pm; Sat 9am-6pm; Sun 10am-6pm.

In a city brimming with Alpine dining establishments, Meierei takes the *Knödel*. Pop in to this casual lunch spot and make way for the local Bugaboo-pushing crowd attracted by the delicious organic fare on offer. Finish off your meal with a mouth-watering rendition of *Kaffee und Strudel*.

Russian Cosmonaut Kitchen

Gagarin

 Knaackstraße 22
+49 30 4428807
bar-gagarin.com
Senefelderplatz **U2**
Open daily 10am-2am.

With a winning 60s-style Sputnik interior, this Russian bistro blends excellent *kraut* with space age *gestalt*. Celebrating the world's first cosmonaut, Yuri Gagarin, the restaurant offers all the Russian classics along with the requisite vodka list. Fuelled by your meat-heavy brunch, you will feel ready to conquer Prenzlauer Berg and worlds beyond!

Coffee Alchemy

No Fire No Glory

 Rykestraße 45
+49 30 28839233
nofirenoglory.de
Senefelderplatz **U2**, Eberswalder
Straße **U2**
Open daily 10am-8pm.

This stylishly aloof Prenzlauer café executes staggeringly good espresso-based drinks in a wood, steel and concrete setting. On warmer days enjoy your brew while reclining in the wilds of the comfy outdoor pavement seating. No Fire works with local roasters Bonanza (p45) and Copenhagen's Coffee Collective to ensure that only the finest, most equitable beans are sourced before being crafted into mesmerising brews.

Luso-Café

Galão A Pastelaria

 Weinbergsweg 8
+49 30 4404 6882
Rosenthaler Platz **U8**
Open daily. Mon-Fri 7.30am-8pm; Sat 8am-8pm; Sun 9am-7pm.

Fancy a warm *pastel de nata* with your *cafezinho*? Then make a beeline for this authentic contemporary Portuguese café flanking the neighbourhood's characteristic tram tracks. A convivial ambiance prevails as a crowd of local followers hit the establishment's Portuguese tiles daily to pick up their coffee fix, along with addictive Iberian pastries and fresh soups and sandwiches. In the summer, enjoy your *galão* outdoors on the café's mint green front-deck chairs.

Sushi Champions

Sasaya

 Lychener Straße 50
+49 30 44717721

sasaya-berlin.de

Eberswalder Straße **U2**,
Schönhauser Allee **S**

Closed Tue/Wed. Open Thu-Mon
noon-3pm, 6pm-11.30pm.

If you're pining for sashimi and soba in a city inclined towards the *Wurst*, make a dash for Sasaya. A contemporary and authentic Japanese restaurant, Sasaya's delectably fresh sushi, meticulous sake list and perfectly frothy *matcha* make this a must for those with Nipponised palates.

Convivial Italian

Pappa e Ciccia

 Schwedter Straße 18
+49 30 61620801

pappaeciccia.de

Senefelderplatz **U2**, Rosenthaler
Platz **U8**

Open daily. Mon from 6pm; Tue-Sun
from 11am.

Prenzlauer Berg's most alluring
Italian merges a convivial rustic-
chic ambiance with tender *piatti*,
bursting with flavour. Ideal for a
cena a due, Pappa also concocts
one of the neighbourhood's
best weekend brunches. Organic
ingredients are sourced whenever
possible and vegan options make
for a light contrast to the typically
meat-and-dairy heavy fare available
around the city.

Friedrichshain

—Left Wing Stronghold

Friedrichshain, a blue-collar inner-city neighbourhood to the east of Mitte, has been a left wing and communist stronghold since its 19th century beginnings. Today it has a markedly countercultural character and its *Kneipen* and second hand shops attract an alternative and mostly young audience.

Named after the vast Volkspark Friedrichshain at its northern fringes, the area developed a distinct identity when it was incorporated into Berlin in 1920. The new district was dominated by the Stralauer Viertel on the edge of Mitte, which had evolved from a rural suburb into an industrial powerhouse with the opening of the Frankfurter Bahnhof, today's Ostbahnhof, in 1842.

During World War II, the Stralauer Viertel was almost entirely destroyed. In its place, East Germany's communist government built Stalinallee (today's Karl-Marx-Allee), a wide socialist-classical boulevard, and site of the *Kosmos*, the former country's largest cinema. The district, filled with concrete blocks of flats, became a showcase socialist neighbourhood. Friedrichshain's outer reaches, left intact by the war, but decaying, avoided this fate. After Berlin's reunification these dense, deserted, pre-war blocks were discovered by squatters and those in search of low rent, laying the foundation for the neighbourhood's alternative character.

Today, pockets of Friedrichshain, especially the attractive pre-war blocks in its eastern part, have seen the arrival of professionals and families. In the south, at its Spree riverbanks, the former Osthafen's warehouses have been taken over by media companies and extensive office and hotel developments.

▲ PRENZLAUER BERG (PAGE 43)

1 Schoenbrunn

VOLKSPARK
FRIEDRICHSHAIN

Landsberger Allee

Mollstr.

Pl. der Vereinten Nationen

FRIEDRICH

Friedenstr.

Schulweg

Palisadenstr.

◀ MITTE (PAGE 11)

U Schillingstraße
U5

Karl-Marx-Allee

U Strausberger Platz
U5
Blumenstr.

5

Singerstr.

Lichtenberger Str.

Singerstr.

Rüdersdorfer S

Holzmarktstr.

Lange Str.

Andreasstr.

Str. der Pariser Kommune

Am Wrie

Wriezener

N

300 metres

▼ KREUZBERG (PAGE 69)

S Ostbahnhof

BERLIN

Enchanted Meal in the Park

Schoenbrunn

1   Am Friedrichshain 8
    +49 30 453056525

schoenbrunn.net

Strausberger Platz **U5**

Open daily 10am-6pm. In winter weekends only.

Tuck into meat-and-potato style Berlin fare amidst the mushrooms and butterflies of Friedrichshain's Volkspark. Schoenbrunn's 60s-style architecture extends onto a Hanna Barbera type white mosaic deck overlooking the surrounding flora—the ultimate venue for a whimsical summer's night out.

East German State Security

Stasi Museum

2 Ruschestraße 103
+49 30 5536854
stasimuseum.de
Magdalenenstraße **U5**
Open daily. Mon-Fri 10am-6pm; Sat/
Sun noon-6pm. Admission €5

The East German dictatorship kept its population in check through one of the most highly effective state security services in history: the Ministry for State Security, commonly known as Stasi. When it was dismantled in 1989, it had a staff of over 90,000, and 2.5% of the country's working age population were employed as informants. The museum is housed in the organisation's former headquarters, and the centrepiece of the exhibition is the preserved office of its former head, Erich Mielke.

Berlin Wall Graffiti

East Side Gallery

 Mühlenstraße
+49 172 3918726
eastsidegallery-berlin.com
Warschauer Straße **U1**, Warschauer
Straße **S**
Public access.

Along the river Spree, at Friedrichshain's former border with West Berlin's Kreuzberg, a section of the Berlin Wall is now an open-air gallery. Painted in 1990, the gallery was the first project of Germany's reunified association of visual artists. It consists of 105 paintings by artists from across the world, documenting the euphoria and hopes of the period. Immediately adjacent, the two neighbourhoods are connected by Oberbaumbrücke, an intricate brick gothic double-deck bridge carrying pedestrian, car and U-Bahn traffic across the Spree River.

An Alpine Fantasy

Schneeweiss

 Simplonstraße 16
+49 30 29049704
schneeweiss-berlin.de
Warschauer Straße **S**,
Samariterstraße **U5**
Open daily. Mon-Fri 6pm-1am; Sat/
Sun 10am-1am.

A nouvelle-Alpine restaurant with a snow white and parquet clad interior, Schneeweiss brings out the glam in Friedrichshain. Join fashionable young couples and media types from nearby Media Spree in the buzzing space, while sipping on one of several excellent Teutonic wines. New spins on classics the likes of *Gulasch* and *Wienerschnitzel* are well worth the trek out to Berlin's far east.

Mid-Century Bar

ČSA Bar

5 Karl-Marx-Allee 96
+49 30 29044741
csa-bar.de
Weberwiese **U5**
Open daily from 8pm.

A retro-futuristic watering hole in the former offices of Czech Airlines on windswept Karl Marx Allee, ČSA's slick and sophisticated interior could come straight off the set of a James Bond flick. The barren grandeur of the area's architecture is redolent of the former East, providing the ultimate snow-dusted backdrop for a cocktail relished over conspiratorial conversation.

Kreuzberg & Neukölln

—Alternative Melting Pot

Kreuzberg, the densely populated inner-city district to the south of Mitte, is famous for its countercultural outlook and high share of immigrant residents, especially from Turkey. Its May Day riots are still a fixture, but squatters have been replaced by a bourgeois populace more concerned with sustainability and ethnic food.

Kreuzberg has a relatively short history. It came into existence when Berlin's tariff walls were moved in the 18th century to capture economic activity in its suburbs. To the south of the city this included large swathes of farmland that were to become Kreuzberg. During Berlin's industrialisation, the area was densely built up with workshops and *Mietskasernen*, Berlin's famous blue-collar architecture with multiple adjoining backyards. Kochstraße, in Kreuzberg's more bourgeois west, evolved into the city's publishing hub. It is still home to both left-wing *taz* and conservative Axel Springer. Berlin's partition left Kreuzberg on the fringes of the West and thus unattractive for investment. The cheap housing stock of its peripheral far east, still known as "SO 36" for its former postcode, were attractive to low income *Gastarbeiter* families and students, artists and alternative types from West Germany.

Berlin's reunification put Kreuzberg back at the centre of the city. The heart of classic countercultural Kreuzberg around Oranienstraße and down to Schlesisches Tor has been discovered by tourists, and its high ceilinged apartment buildings by a more bourgeois set, pushing artists and students south into formerly notorious Neukölln. The attractive area between the two, now known as "Kreuzkölln", has become an interesting mix of cafés, restaurants and artist's ateliers.

▲ UNTER DEN LINDEN (PAGE 31)

Waldemarstr.

Adalbertstr.

Waldemarstr.

U Moritzplatz
U8

Prinzessinenstr.

Oranienstr.

KREUZBERG

Prinzenstr.

Bergfriedstr.

Ritterstr.

Kottbusser Tor **U**
U1/U8

Skalitzer Str.

Gilschiner Str.

Manteuffelstr.

U Prinzenstraße
U1

UNTER DEN LINDEN(PAGE 31)

7 Landwehrkanal

Planufer

Böckhstr.

Schinkestr.

Graefestr.

6 Kadó

Burknerstr.

U Schönleinstraße
U8

Süper Store **5**

Dieffenbachstr.

Sanderstr.

4 Flughafen Tempelhof

Urbanstr.

Boppstr.

Pilügerstr.

Hobrechtstr.

Körtestr.

Fichtelstr.

Kottbusser Damm

Lenaustr.

Jahnstr.

N

300 metres

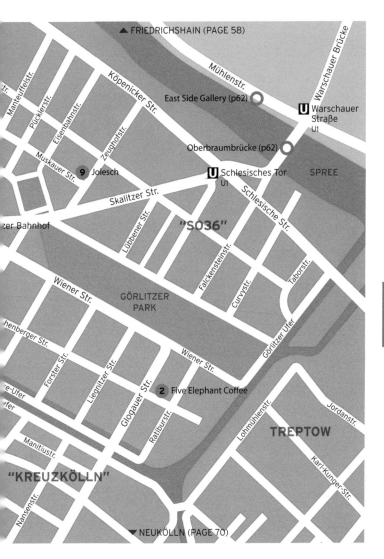

▲ FRIEDRICHSHAIN (PAGE 58)

Manteuffelstr.

Köpenicker Str.

Pücklerstr.

Eisenbahnstr.

East Side Gallery (p62)

Mühlenstr.

Warschauer Brücke

U Warschauer Straße
U1

Zeughofstr.

Muskauer Str.

Oberbraumbrücke (p62)

9 Jolesch

U Schlesisches Tor
U1

SPREE

Skalitzer Str.

zer Bahnhof

Lübbener Str.

Schlesische Str.

"SO36"

Falckensteinstr.

Wiener Str.

Taborstr.

GÖRLITZER PARK

Curvystr.

henberger Str.

Görlitzer Ufer

Forster Str.

Liegnitzer Str.

Wiener Str.

Glogauer Str.

2 Five Elephant Coffee

e-Ufer

Lohmühlenstr.

Jordanstr.

fer

Ratiburstr.

Manitiustr.

TREPTOW

Karl-Kunger-Str.

"KREUZKÖLLN"

Nansenstr.

▼ NEUKÖLLN (PAGE 70)

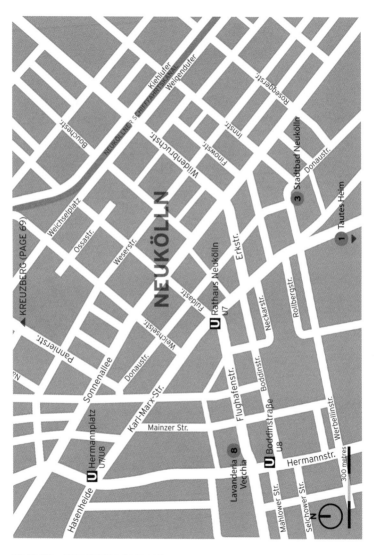

Horseshoe Estate

Tautes Heim

 Located in the Hufeisensiedlung
estate on Parchimer Allee;
details upon request

+49 30 60107193

tautes-heim.de

Parchimer Allee **U7**

Entire residence (2 bedrooms) from
€150/night incl. tax

Tautes Heim is a modernist town house set within Bruno Taut's lush and highly innovative 1920s Hufeisensiedlung (Horseshoe) estate. Created as a response to workers' squalid housing conditions at the time, the estate sought to marry urban life with rural ideals in a functional, but aesthetically pleasing package. Tautes Heim has been meticulously restored with original fixtures and 1930s furniture affording guests unique insight into Berlin's social and architectural history.

Kiez Café

Five Elephant Coffee

 Reichenberger Straße 101
+49 30 96081527
fiveelephant.com
Görlitzer Bahnhof **U1**
Open daily. Mon-Fri 8.30am-7pm;
Sat/Sun 10am-7pm.

A coffee highlight in this at once patchy and elegant stretch of residential Kreuzberg, Five Elephant Coffee roasts its own beans with staggeringly potent results. Herringbone parquet and a giant vintage world map outlining coffee regions near and far complement the establishment's high ceilings and cosy installations. The ideal spot to warm up with a cappuccino and cake on a cold winter's day.

A Morning Dip

Stadtbad Neukölln

 Ganghoferstraße 3
+49 30 6824980

berlinerbaeder.de

Rathaus Neukölln **U7**, Karl-Marx-Straße **U7**

Opening hours vary, refer to website.
Admission €4.50

Inspired by the thermal baths of the ancient world and boasting travertine columns and intricate mosaics, the Stadtbad Neukölln is perhaps the most glamorous public swimming pool in operation today. Inaugurated in 1914, its neoclassical building originally encompassed both a public swimming pool and a public library, envisioned to combine both physical and mental exercise in a single locale. The bath consists of two pool halls as well as a sauna.

Monumentalist Architecture

Flughafen Tempelhof

 Platz der Luftbrücke 5
tempelhoferfreiheit.de
Platz der Luftbrücke **U6**
Tours of the buildings available,
refer to website for programme.
Admission €12.
Park open from dawn to dusk.

Though no longer in operation today, Tempelhof Airport is the cradle of modern aviation in Germany and intimately interlinked with Berlin's history. In the 1930s, Germany's Nazi government set out to rebuild it as a monumental new gateway to Berlin. Among the largest buildings of its time, Tempelhof's terminal with its canopy style roof provided adequate facilities until well into the 1970s. During the 1948/49 Berlin blockade, Tempelhof was West Berlin's only connection to the outside world. The airport was closed in 2008 and its airfield will be converted into a park.

Fabulous Gifts

Süper Store

 Dieffenbachstraße 12
+49 30 98327944
sueper-store.de
Schönleinstraße **U8**,
Kottbusser Tor **U1** **U8**
Closed Sun/Mon. Open Tue-Fri 11am-7pm; Sat 11am-4pm.

Tucked away in the midst of Kreuzberg's charming Graefekiez area, Süper Store gathers artisanally crafted sustainable *objets trouvés* from across the globe. Drop by after an invigorating stroll along nearby Landwehrkanal (p77) and pick up a pair of Furlane slippers, a copper Ottoman-style Turkish hammam water bowl or a bottle of locally distilled Our/Berlin Vodka among the panoply of exotic and refined items. Highly recommended for finding a unique gift or two.

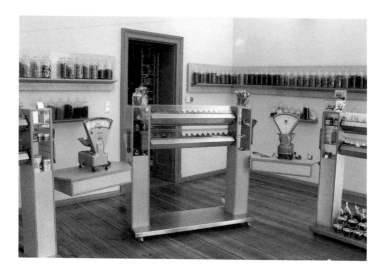

Liquorice Shop

Kadó

 Graefestraße 20
+49 30 69041638
kado.de
Schönleinstraße **U8**
Closed Sun/Mon. Open Tue-Fri
9.30am-6.30pm; Sat 9.30am-
3.30pm.

Purveyors of the finest liquorice since 1997, Kadó offers a dazzling range of the sweet treat. With over four hundred varieties hailing from Iceland to Sicily in a multiplicity of shapes, textures and colours, Kado will fulfil the liquorice fantasies of even the most savoury tooth. The pine and glass sweet jar aesthetic pairs perfectly with the exquisite confectionery on offer.

Canal-Side Life

Landwehrkanal

7 between Kottbusser Str and
Ratiborstraße
Schönleinstraße **U8**, Görlitzer
Bahnhof **U1**
Public access.

Berlin is crisscrossed by a number
canals built in the 19th century to
link factories and warehouses to
markets further afield. Today the
canals are almost exclusively used
for leisure activities. Completed in
1850, the Landwehr Canal runs the
length of Kreuzberg, connecting
Friedrichshain with Charlottenburg.
Its tree lined paths, notably the
Paul-Lincke-Ufer, invite strolls along
the water with coffee and beer
breaks along the way.

Canteen to Fine Dining

Lavanderia Vecchia

 Flughafenstraße 46
+49 30 62722152
lavanderiavecchia.de
Boddinstraße **U8**, Rathaus
Neukölln **U7**
Closed Sun/Mon. Lunch Tue-Fri
noon-2.30pm. Dinner Tue-Sat from
7.30pm (reservation only).

Step into the picturesque courtyard
surrounding Lavanderia Vecchia
and enter a parallel world to this
otherwise crusty patch of Neukölln.
At lunchtime, media and artsy
types jostle for space at one of the
restaurant's convivial communal
tables as waiters whizz by with
today's fresh *primi* and *secondi*.
Dinner is an altogether more
upscale and intimate affair, with a
reservations-only policy and a top-
notch Italian set menu on offer.

Prime Gulasch

Jolesch

 Muskauer Straße 1
+49 30 6123581
jolesch.de
Görlitzer Bahnhof **U1**
Open daily. Mon-Fri 11.30am-midnight; Sat/Sun 10am-midnight.

An Austrian classic with a twist, Jolesch cooks up an Alpine storm to scores of Kreuzberg fans of *Gulasch* and *Sachertorte*. The main dining room keeps up the façade with its regal sienna and green walls looming atop herringbone parquet leading up to a tumultuous depiction of a storm at sea. A mountain of glorious cakes sits squarely at the centre of the space, luring diners on a precipitous course towards desert. In summer months the fun spills out onto Jolesch's streetside terrace.

Charlottenburg

—Royal Residence and West Berlin Bling

Founded as a blue blooded *Residenzstadt* on the opposite side of the Tiergarten park from Berlin proper, wealthy Charlottenburg has, over time, played a variety of roles as Mitte's counterpart and rival. The district was West Berlin's commercial and social centre during the Cold War, but its star has faded with the revival of Berlin's historic centre. Its leafy streets and generous *Gründerzeit* architecture are home to Berlin's moneyed and professional classes.

Charlottenburg was founded by Frederick I of Prussia in 1705 at the site of a hamlet across from a palace commissioned by his wife, Charlotte. The town became popular with wealthy Berliners, first for recreation, and later as residence. In the late 19th century, the then "richest town in Prussia" established lavish public institutions: the Deutsche Oper, its grand town hall and famed universities. Residents like Werner von Siemens built flourishing businesses, and the Kurfürstendamm became the "New West", Berlin's centre of leisure and nightlife during the Golden Twenties. The momentum continued with Berlin's Cold War partition, which left Mitte inaccessible behind the Wall in Soviet East Berlin and Charlottenburg at the centre of a heavily subsidised West Berlin. Much wealth found its way to Tauentzienstraße and Breitscheidplatz, site of both the war-damaged Kaiser Wilhelm Memorial Church and the Europa-Center's characteristic revolving Mercedes-Benz star.

Having already lost its avant-garde edge to multicultural Kreuzberg in the 1970s and 80s, Charlottenburg suffered from the revival of Mitte as a shopping and entertainment district after Berlin's reunification. Nevertheless, its distinct upper-class caché, acquired over generations, has preserved its popularity with a conservative, well-heeled and sophisticated clientele.

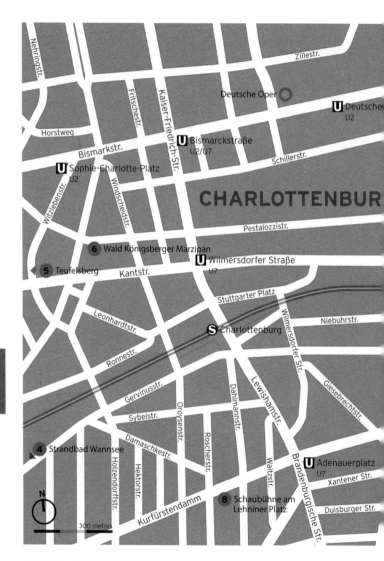

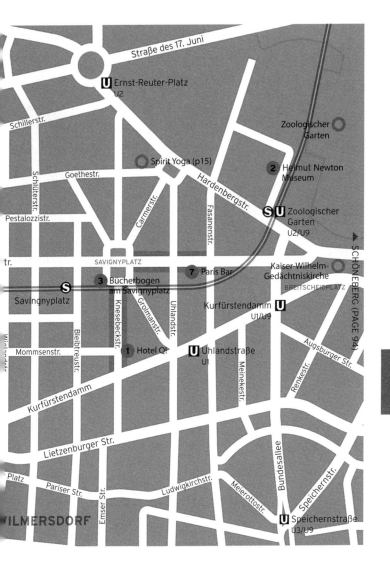

Straße des 17. Juni

U Ernst-Reuter-Platz
U2

Schillerstr.

Schlüterstr.

Pestalozzistr.

Goethestr.

Carmerstr.

Spirit Yoga (p15)

Zoologischer Garten

2 Helmut Newton Museum

Hardenbergstr.

Fasanenstr.

S U Zoologischer Garten
U2/U9

tr.

SAVIGNYPLATZ

7 Paris Bar

Kaiser-Wilhelm-Gedächtniskirche

BREITSCHEIDPLATZ

S Savingnyplatz

3 Bücherbogen am Savignyplatz

Knesebeckstr.

Grolmanstr.

Uhlandstr.

Kurfürstendamm **U**
U1/U9

Wielandstr.

Bleibtreustr.

Mommsenstr.

1 Hotel Q!

U Uhlandstraße
U1

Meinekestr.

Augsburger Str.

Renkestr.

SCHÖNEBERG (PAGE 94)

Kurfürstendamm

Lietzenburger Str.

Platz

Pariser Str.

Emser Str.

Ludwigkirchstr.

Meierottostr.

Bundesallee

Speichernstr.

ILMERSDORF

U Speichernstraße
U3/U9

Futuristic Lodgings

Hotel Q!

1 Knesebeckstraße 33-34
+49 30 81825720
qhotelsresorts.com
Uhlandstraße **U1**, Savignyplatz **S**
Doubles from €120/night incl. tax

A futuristic boutique lodging with a distinct Charlottenburg vibe. The self-described rock star of a hotel was designed by GRAFT-architects who styled the space with unique elements such as artificial ostrich leather and baked oak. Adding to the hedonistic whimsy, the hotel's spa incorporates heated sand and a Japanese-style washing zone and sauna. The space's rocket ship aesthetic has not diminished the comfort of the well-appointed rooms. Q! is a ludic urban pad from which to explore West Berlin and beyond.

Helmut Newton Foundation, Berlin 2012; copyright Stephan Müller

Photography Icon

Helmut Newton Museum

 Jebensstraße 2
+49 30 31864856
helmutnewton.com
Zoologischer
Garten **S** **U2** **U9**
Closed Mon. Open Tue/Wed/Fri-Sun 10am-6pm; Thu 10am-8pm. Admission €10

Iconic photographer Helmut Newton changed the face of nude photography with his pioneering, overblown black-and-white work. The Helmut Newton Museum displays an extensive range of the artist's best photographs, along with his cameras, a reconstruction of his workspace and videos outlining his trajectory from Berlin to Australia, to his career at *Vogue*. Housed in the monumental former Landwehrkasino, the museum's setting lives up to its content. If you'd rather admire the nudes while sipping on a martini, head to the Newton Bar (p39) where several originals are on permanent display.

Visual Bookshop

Bücherbogen am Savignyplatz

 Stadtbahnbogen 593
+49 30 31869511
buecherbogen.com
Savignyplatz **S**, Uhlandstraße **U1**
Closed Sun. Open Mon-Fri 10am-8pm; Sat 10am-6pm.

Tucked under the arches beneath the *Stadtbahn* rail tracks along elegant Savignyplatz, Bücherbogen is a renowned specialty bookshop focusing on architecture, art, photography, film, design and antiques. Mounds of gorgeous coffee table books vie for space with the latest publications and visual media classics. If you've been inspired by the offerings, head over for more at the neighbouring Helmut Newton Museum (p85).

Lake Beach

Strandbad Wannsee

 Wannseebadweg 25
+49 30 787325
strandbadwannsee.de
Nikolasee Ⓢ
Open daily from late Mar to late Sep.
High season Mon-Fri 9am-8pm; Sat/
Sun 8am-9pm. Admission €4.50

The Strandbad Wannsee is an open-air lido on the forested eastern shore of the Wannsee lake, landlocked Berlin's ersatz sea. As the largest inland lido in Europe it boasts over 1km of sandy beach, naturally dotted with Germany's famous *Strandkörbe* ("beach baskets") to offer sheltered seating. The site was a popular bathing spot as far back as the prudish 19th century, and its sprawling New Objectivity facilities date from the 1920s. Decayed after decades of cheap air travel, a painstaking restoration of the lido began in the mid 2000s.

Communications Ruins

Teufelsberg

 Teufelsseechaussee
+49 163 8585096
berlinsightout.de
Heerstraße Ⓢ
Regular tours. Refer to website for programme.

The Teufelsberg rises 80 metres above the surrounding Grunewald forest to the west of Charlottenburg. The hill was heaped up when the streets of West Berlin were cleared of war rubble. During the Cold War, the US National Security Agency built a large listening station on top of the hill. After the fall of the Wall, the equipment was removed, but the buildings and radar domes remained. Freely accessible until only four years ago, the privately-owned site has remained open to the public for tours and, more recently, art installations.

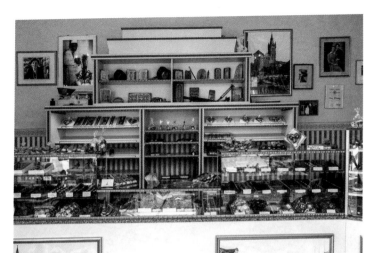

Marzipan Specialist

Wald Königsberger Marzipan

6 Pestalozzistraße 54a
+49 30 3238254
wald-koenigsberger-marzipan.de
Sophie-Charlotte-Platz **U2**,
Charlottenburg **S**, Wilmersdorfer
Straße **U7**
Closed Sun. Open Mon-Fri 10am-
6.30pm; Sat 10am-3.30pm.

An exceptional purveyor of the almond-based delight, Wald Königsberger Marzipan was once the purveyor of choice to the Prussian nobility. The quality of Wald's marzipan-based loaves, squares and chocolates pay testament to the house's regal roots. Established in Charlottenburg by Paul Wald and his wife and master confectioner Irmgard Radant in 1947, the shop is now overseen by the third generation of Berliner Walds.

Classic West Berlin

Paris Bar

7 Kantstraße 152
+49 30 3138052
parisbar.net
Uhlandstraße **U1**, Zoologischer
Garten **S** **U2** **U9**
Open daily noon-1am.

A stalwart on the Berlin scene since the 1960's, theatrical French bistro-style Paris Bar is still the regular haunt of artists, celebrities and those generally leading la *vie bohème*, and is open late enough to fulfil midnight steak-au-poivre and pommard cravings. The restaurant exudes retro *je ne sais quoi* and buzzes into the wee hours of the morning. The artwork adorning its walls are the creations of its faithful clientele, garnered over decades of cuisine and intellect.

Engaged Theatre

Schaubühne am Lehniner Platz

8 Kurfürstendamm 153
+49 30 890023
schaubuehne.de
Adenauerplatz **U7**,
Charlottenburg **S**
Regular performances. Refer to
website for programme.

The ever avant-garde award winning Schaubühne am Lehniner Platz was founded by a group of socially engaged theatre enthusiasts in 1962. True to its roots, the theatre's repertoire continues to explore the workings behind social and political marginalisation in its blend of classics and modern masterpieces from Ibsen to Caryl Churchill and Lars Norén. From its 60s-style auditorium, the Schaubühne acts as a laboratory for the exploration of the transformations and fissures engendered by Berlin's re-unification.

Schöneberg

—West Berlin Bourgeousie

Schöneberg, like Charlottenburg a wealthy former suburb of Berlin, has a distinctly more democratic and intellectual feel than its more uptight neighbour to the northwest. Its central parts around Nollendorfplatz have been at the centre of gay life in Berlin since the 1920s, during Germany's progressive Weimar Republic. Schöneberg's quieter south is dominated by imposing *Gründerzeit* buildings and its squares host comprehensive weekly farmers markets.

The hamlet of "villa sconenberch" was mentioned as early as 1264 but retained its bucolic character until being engulfed by thriving Berlin in the 1870s. In 1919, Schöneberg had a population of 175,000 and the next year it was incorporated into Berlin. "Millionaire farmers" cashed in on their land and developers built elaborate new neighbourhoods for prospective upper class residents. Most notable was the Bayerisches Viertel, which was popular with Berlin's Jewish intelligentsia, among them Albert Einstein. Destroyed in World War II air raids, the area was rebuilt in utilitarian 1950s style. Schöneberg was also Germany's second city, after Berlin, to build a metro, today the Berlin metro's U4. During the Cold War, Schöneberg's town hall served as town hall for West Berlin and was the site of John F. Kennedy's famous "Ich bin ein Berliner" speech.

Schöneberg's north is part of Berlin's busy City West shopping district, also site of the KaDeWe, the largest department store in continental Europe. The remainder of the district has led a relatively low-key existence since Berlin's reunification. Much of the action during the past twenty years has taken place in Berlin's former east, leaving Schöneberg relatively untouched. Its bars tend to be unpretentious, its cafes welcoming and its markets exude a friendly neighbourhood feel.

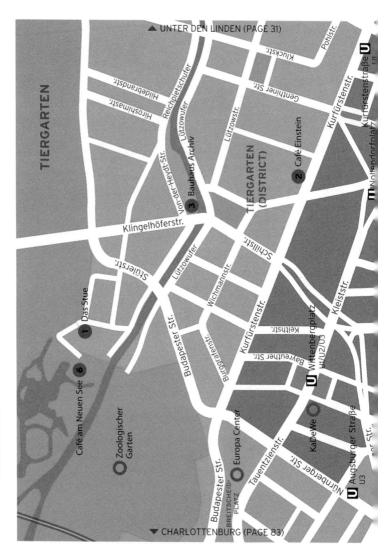

▲ UNTER DEN LINDEN (PAGE 31)

TIERGARTEN

Pohlstr.

Kluckstr.

Genthiner Str.

Kurfürstenstr.

Hildebrandstr.

Reichpietschufer

Hiroshimastr.

Lützowufer

Lützowstr.

Kurfürstenstraße U

Von-der-Heydt-Str.

3 Bauhaus Archiv

2 Café Einstein

Nollendorfplatz U

TIERGARTEN (DISTRICT)

Klingelhöferstr.

Schillstr.

Stülerstr.

Lützowufer

Wichmannstr.

Kleiststr.

1 Das Stue

Budapester Str.

Burggrafenstr.

Kurfürstenstr.

Keithstr.

Kurfürstenstr.

Wittenbergplatz U1/U2/U3

Bayreuther Str.

6 Café am Neuen See

Zoologischer Garten

Augsburger Straße U3

Europa Center

KaDeWe

Tauentzienstr.

Nürnberger Str.

...er Str.

Budapester Str.

BREITSCHEID-PLATZ

▼ CHARLOTTENBURG (PAGE 83)

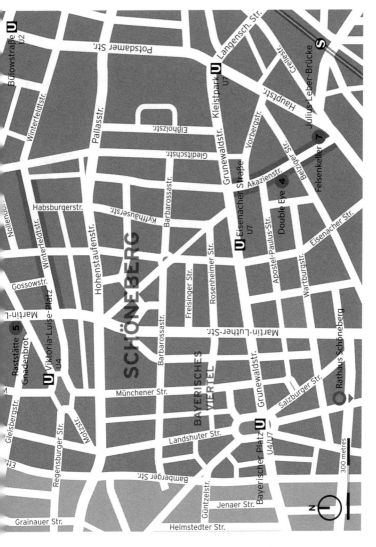

Tiergarten Hotel

Das Stue

 Drakestraße 1
+49 30 311 7220
das-stue.com
Wittenbergplatz **U1 U2 U3**,
Tiergarten **S**
Doubles from €200/night incl. tax

Located in the upmarket Tiergarten neighbourhood on the edge of the eponymous park, meticulously appointed Das Stue exudes laissez-faire elegance. Spanish designer Patricia Urquiola envisioned a luxurious house for the 80-room hotel, melding the spirit of the building's 1930s architecture with more contemporary nuances inspired by the fauna of the Berlin Zoo, which Das Stue overlooks. All rooms are unique, some including a terrace and others with views over the Tiergarten and the zoo.

Mitteleuropean Café House

Café Einstein

2 Kurfürstenstraße 58
+49 30 263919
cafeeinstein.com
Nollendorfplatz **U1 U2 U3 U4**
Open daily 8am-1am.

The original *Stammhaus* of this Berlin coffee classic, Café Einstein's majestic turn-of-the-century *Kaffeehaus* setting adds Mitteleuropean splendour to your espresso. Cosy up on one of the leather banquettes with a slice of the latest newspaper and brunch with all the trimmings before heading out to explore Schöneberg's eclectic offerings. Café Einstein is open late into the night and continues to serve breakfast until closing.

Modernist Architecture

Bauhaus Archiv

 Klingelhöferstraße 14
+49 30 2540
bauhaus.de
Nollendorfplatz U1 U2 U3 U4
Closed Tue. Open Wed-Mon 10am-5pm. Admission €7

Founded in 1960, the Bauhaus Archiv is dedicated to the collection of art pieces and literature related to the Bauhaus design school. Operating during the 1920s Weimar Republic, the school was one of the most influential precursors to modern design and architecture. The museum's building, finished in 1979, is based on a design by Walter Gropius. The collection includes teaching materials, workshop models and drawings. It also documents the school's impact on art, design and architecture.

Neighbourhood Café

Double Eye

 Akazienstraße 22
+49 179 4566960

doubleeye.de

Eisenacher Straße **U7**, Julius-Leber-Brücke **S**

Closed Sun. Open Mon-Fri 9.30am-6.30pm; Sat 10am-3.30pm.

Prominently announced from Akazienstrasse by its standout double eye logo, this espresso bar is not to be missed. A favourite of the local intelligentsia and cappuccino sipping crowd, Double Eye provides top-flight espresso based drinks to the discerning customer. During the summer months, the crowd, their dogs and lattes, all spill out onto the street for caffeine-fuelled banter.

Unconventional Pub

Raststätte Gnadenbrot

5 Martin-Luther-Straße 20A
+49 30 21961786
raststaette-gnadenbrot.de
Viktoria-Luise-Platz **U4**,
Wittenbergplatz **U1 U2 U3**
Open daily from 9am.

An unusual mix of maritime influences and mid-century kitsch, Raststätte Gnadenbrot is a wildly playful restaurant and bar. Located on a rather bland stretch of Schöneberg carriageway, Raststätte delights with its eccentric interior and extensive breakfast menu. Dinner is a decidedly local affair, with *Kraut*, *Wurst* and *Bratkartoffeln* all making steadfast appearances.

Beer Garden by the Lake

Café am Neuen See

 Lichtensteinallee 2
+49 30 25449300
cafe-am-neuen-see.de

Tiergarten Ⓢ,
Wittenbergplatz **U1 U2 U3**
Open daily from 9am. Beer garden
Mon-Fri from 11am; Sat/Sun from
10am.

Set by a lake in the thick of the Tiergarten, Café am Neuen See provides enchanting surroundings to accompany a lakeside meal *al fresco*. The casual dining menu includes several Germanic and Italian classics, but the view is what you'll remember. If you're in this neck of the woods and looking for a fresh draught beer, Café am Neuen See also has a *Biergarten*, directly overlooking the lake.

Neighbourhood Kneipe

Felsenkeller

 Akazienstraße 2
+49 30 7813447
Julius-Leber-Brücke Ⓢ, Eisenacher
Straße Ⓤ7
Closed Sun. Open Mon-Fri 4pm-1am;
Sat noon-2am.

A classic Schöneberg *Kneipe* with a maritime interior and a constantly jovial flow of beer on tap, Felsenkeller is the place to go to experience timeless West Berlin. The crowd is a mix of neighbourhood locals and cosmopolitan visitors enjoying the Homemade Herring Salad and other down-to-earth classics in the refreshingly smoke-free setting.

Essentials

Airport Transfer

Ever since re-becoming Germany's capital in 1998 there have been plans to consolidate Berlin's airports at one site. The opening of the new Berlin Brandenburg Airport (BER), a major upgrade to the current Schönefeld Airport (see below), was scheduled for 2010 but has now been delayed to 2014 or later.

Tegel (TXL): Berlin's main airport does not have a rail connection, but its central location makes it easily accessible by taxi. A taxi ride from Mitte's Friedrichstraße will cost €20-25 and take around 20 minutes. There are *JetExpressBus* airport express buses to Alexanderplatz (30-40 mins, via Hauptbahnhof) and Bahnhof Zoo (20 mins). Standard public transport tickets are valid on these buses.

Schönefeld (SFX): Formerly East Berlin's capital airport, Schönefeld lies in the city's outskirts, making taxis pricier than most of the low-cost flights that land there. A taxi ride to Friedrichstraße will cost around €45-50 and take 30-40 minutes. The airport's station is served by *AirportExpress* trains to stations across the city centre, which depart twice an hour and take 28 minutes to Hauptbahnhof. S-Bahn commuter trains leave on 20-minute intervals to neighbourhoods in the city's south (S45) and east (S9). Standard public transport tickets (Zone C, €3.10) are valid on all trains to and from the airport.

Taxis

Berlin's taxis, many of them Germany's classic beige Mercedes-Benz variety, are a fairly common sight on the city's main thoroughfares, especially in Mitte and Charlottenburg. However, taxis are not as innate a part of metropolitan life as they are in, say, New York. Berlin is more spread out and fares are higher. Hauptbahnhof to Prenzlauer Berg will cost €10-15 and take around 15 mins. Crossing the city centre is usually quick but can cost €30 or more. The most common service for advance bookings is Funk Taxi (+49 30 261026). Many taxis do not accept credit cards.

Public Transport

Opened in 1902, Berlin's U-Bahn ("underground railway") is an efficient and reliable way to cover ground in central Berlin. Trains operate from around 4am to 12.30am, depending on day and line. Trains depart every 5 minutes, with more regular intervals during peak hours, and less regular at night. Most lines operate on quarter-hourly schedule throughout Friday and Saturday nights.

The U-Bahn is complemented by the commuter train type S-Bahn operated by Germany's national rail operator. Its main east-west *Stadtbahn* trunk provides a quick link between Mitte and Charlottenburg. In addition, the neighbourhoods of former East Berlin, including Prenzlauer Berg and Friedrichshain, are covered by a dense tram network.

All public transport in Berlin shares a single fare structure with three fare zones. All areas covered in this book are located in Zone A, Tegel Airport in Zone B and Schönefeld Airport in Zone C. Single tickets cost €2.40 across Zone A+B and €3.10 across Zones A-C. Day passes for Zones A+B cost €6.50 and weekly passes €28. Refer to p110 for a map of the Berlin U-Bahn and S-Bahn.

Tipping

Germany's tipping culture lies somewhere half way between America and southern Europe. Tips are not required, but they are usually expected. Unless the service is abhorrent, tip 5-10% in restaurants and taxis and round up in cafés.

Safety

Generally safe, Berlin is a major city that has punched below its weight prosperity wise for a few decades, leaving it with its share of rough patches. On a very a high level, the city's southwest is prosperous and safe. Incidents are more likely to occur in the economically deprived inner-city neighbourhoods (such as Neukölln) and far eastern suburbs.

Index

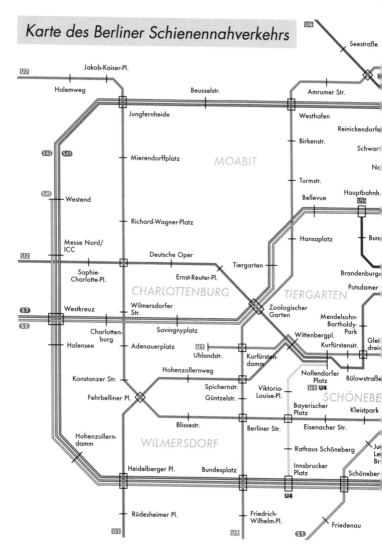

Karte des Berliner Schienennahverkehrs

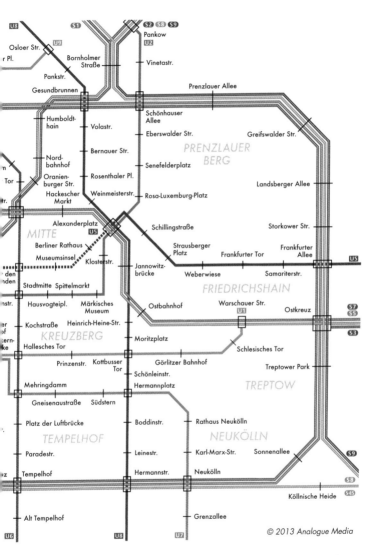

© 2013 Analogue Media

Credits

Published by Analogue Media, LLC
244 5th Avenue, Suite 2446, New York, NY 10001, United States

Edited by Alana Stone
Layout & Production by Stefan Horn

For more information about the Analogue Guides series, or to find out about availability and purchase information, please visit analogueguides.com

First Edition 2013
ISBN: 978-0-9838585-4-6

Typefaces: Neutraface 2, Myriad Pro and Interstate
Paper: Munken Lynx

Printed in Barcelona by Agpograf, S.A.

Analogue Media would like to thank all contributing venues, designers, manufacturers, agencies and photographers for their kind permission to reproduce their work in this book.

Cover design by Dustin Wallace
Proofread by John Leisure

Photography credits: all images credited to the listed venues unless stated otherwise. (9) Stefan Horn (13/15) Steve Herud (16) Fette Sans (17) www. buchstabenmuseum.de Photo: Hendrik Kluender (18) Achim Hatzius (19) Katja Eydel (21/22) Steve Herud (23) Emanuele Pagni (24) Stefan Korte (25) Steve Herud (27) Daniel Rieter (32) Gavin Bloys (33) © Staatliche Museen zu Berlin. Foto: Maximilian Meisse (34) NOSHE (35) © Staatliche Museen zu Berlin, Nationalgalerie, Foto: Achim Kleuker (37) © Schirmer / Berliner Philharmoniker (39) Steve Herud (41) Alana Stone (45) Steve Herud (47) Eldad Carin / Shutterstock.com (48/50/51/52/53/54) Steve Herud (60) Steve Herud (61) John Steer (62) Ppictures (64) Thorsten Klapsch (67) Stefan Horn (73) © Copyright Berliner Bäder-Betriebe (74) Stefan Horn (75) Florian Wenningkamp (76) Dirk Soboll (77) Steve Herud (78) Sabine Münch (81) Stefan Horn (84) Dirk Schaper (85) Helmut Newton Foundation, Berlin 2012, copyright Stephan Müller (86/87) Steve Herud (88) Tobias Beidermühle (89/90) Steve Herud (91) © Thorsten Elger (93) Stefan Horn (97) Steve Herud (98) Bauhaus-Archiv Berlin/ Photo: Hartwig Klappert (99/100/101/102) Steve Herud.

About the Series

—A Modern Take on Simple Elegance

Analogue Guides is a series of curated city guidebooks featuring high quality, unique, low key venues—distilled through the lens of the neighbourhood.

Each neighbourhood is complemented by a concise set of sophisticated listings, including restaurants, cafés, bars, hotels and serendipitous finds, all illustrated with photographs. The listings are supplemented by custom designed, user-friendly maps to facilitate navigation of the cityscape. Venues featured in the guides score high on a number of factors, including locally sourced food, tasteful design, a sophisticated and relaxed atmosphere and independent ownership.

Analogue Guides are designed to complement the internet during pre-travel preparation and smartphones for on-the-ground research. Premium photography and a select choice of venues provide an ideal starting point for pre-travel inspiration. At your destination, the guides serve as portable manuals with detailed neighbourhood maps and clear directions.

The result: a compact, efficient, effervescent manual celebrating the ingenuity of the contemporary metropolis.